BACHELORS COOKBOOK

90 + Easy Recipes

By RB Enterprise

As a bachelor, it can be hard to find
the time and motivation to
cook healthy, tasty meals for yourself.
That's where this cookbook comes in!
"Bachelors Cookbook" is filled with
quick and easy recipes that are
perfect for the busy single cook.
In this cookbook, you'll
find a variety of dishes
that are perfect for any occasion,
whether you're in the mood for a
hearty dinner, a quick lunch,
or just want to try something new.
All of the recipes are simple to follow
and use common ingredients that
are easy to find at your local grocery store.
These recipes can be easily doubled or tripled if you want to feed
more people or have leftovers

So grab a skillet, a pot,
or a baking sheet,
and get ready to cook up a storm with
"Bachelors Cookbook"!

Introduction

Chapter 1: Breakfast

Scrambled eggs with spinach and feta
Avocado toast with scrambled eggs
Greek yogurt with berries and honey
Peanut butter and banana smoothie
Breakfast burrito with scrambled eggs and veggies
Omelet with mushrooms, peppers, and onions
English muffin with ham and cheese
Blueberry pancakes
Quinoa bowls with eggs, veggies, and avocado
Breakfast sandwich with bacon, egg, and cheese
Smoothie bowl with yogurt, berries, and granola
French toast with fresh fruit
Breakfast potatoes with eggs and bacon
Yogurt parfait with granola and fruit
Breakfast hash with sweet potatoes, bacon, and eggs
Bagel with tomato, avocado and bacon
Breakfast pizza with sausage, egg, and cheese
Chia seed pudding with almond milk and fruit
Oatmeal with nuts, seeds, and dried fruit
Breakfast wrap with sausage, egg, and cheese

Chapter 2: Lunch

Grilled chicken Caesar salad
Turkey and cheese wrap with avocado and tomato
Tuna salad sandwich
Black bean and sweet potato burrito
Greek salad with grilled chicken
Quinoa and veggie stir-fry
Turkey burger with sweet potato fries
Spinach and feta omelet
Broccoli and cheddar soup
Chicken and vegetable curry
Turkey chili with avocado
Grilled chicken and veggie kabobs
Turkey meatloaf with roasted vegetables
BBQ Chicken sandwich
Turkey and cheese quesadilla
Grilled chicken and vegetable pasta
Turkey and avocado lettuce cups
Turkey and cheese melt with tomato soup
Turkey and veggie stir fry with brown rice
Turkey and cheese panini with pesto

Chapter 3: Appetizers

Deviled Eggs
Guacamole and Chips
Caprese Salad Skewers
Cheesy Garlic Bread
Baked Brie
Cream Cheese Stuffed Jalapenos
Stuffed Mushrooms
Mini Meatballs
Spinach and Feta Spanakopita
Prosciutto Wrapped Melon
Cucumber and Dill Tea Sandwiches
Fried Green Beans
Buffalo Chicken Dip
Shrimp Cocktail
Smoked Salmon and Cream Cheese
Pesto and Ricotta Crostini
Tzatziki and Pita Chips
Marinated Olives
Pepperoni and Cheese Roll-Ups
Baked Parmesan Garlic Fries

Chapter 4: Dinner

One-pan roasted chicken and vegetables
Skillet beef and broccoli
Grilled cheese and tomato soup
Spaghetti with marinara sauce
Meatball sub
BBQ pulled pork sandwich
Baked salmon with lemon and herbs
Crispy chicken tenders with honey mustard dipping sauce
Chicken and vegetable stir-fry
Baked salmon with a honey mustard glaze
Cheddar and broccoli omelet
Creamy chicken and mushroom pasta
Beef burritos with salsa
Chicken fajitas
Spinach and Monterrey Jack Cheese Omelet
Chicken Fettuccini Noodles
Lemon and herb baked chicken breast
Chicken Parmesan
Baked macaroni and cheese with bacon
Ground Meat chili with Cracker

Chapter 5: Desserts

Chocolate chip cookies
Apple crisp
Banana bread
Chocolate mousse
Berry sorbet
Lemon bars
Brownies
Peach cobbler
Chocolate covered strawberries
Cheesecake
Microwave mug cake
No-bake chocolate peanut butter bars
Berries with yogurt
Strawberry ice cream
Chocolate covered banana
Lemon poppy seed muffins

Chapter 1: Breakfast

Scrambled Eggs with Spinach and Feta

Ingredients:
2 large eggs
Salt and pepper, to taste
1 tsp butter or oil
1 cup fresh spinach
2 tbsp crumbled feta cheese

Directions:
Crack the eggs into a small bowl and beat them with a fork or whisk. Season with salt and pepper.
In a small skillet over medium heat, melt the butter or heat the oil.
Add the spinach to the skillet and cook until it begins to wilt, about 1-2 minutes.
Pour the beaten eggs into the skillet and stir gently with a spatula until the eggs are cooked through, about 2-3 minutes.
Remove the skillet from the heat and stir in the feta cheese.
Serve and enjoy your breakfast, lunch or dinner.
Optional: You can add diced tomatoes, onions or mushrooms to the skillet with the spinach before adding the eggs. And you could also add some hot sauce or pepper flakes for a bit of heat.

This recipe can be easily doubled or tripled if you want to feed more people or have leftovers.

Chapter 1: Breakfast

Avocado toast with scrambled eggs

Ingredients:
2 large eggs
Salt and pepper, to taste
1 tsp butter or oil
1 ripe avocado
2 slices of bread
Optional: cherry tomatoes, hot sauce or pepper flakes

Directions:
Crack the eggs into a small bowl and beat them with a fork or whisk.
Season with salt and pepper.
Heat a small skillet over medium heat and add the butter or oil.
Pour the beaten eggs into the skillet and stir gently with a spatula until the eggs are cooked through, about 2-3 minutes.
Remove the skillet from the heat.
While the eggs are cooking, mash the avocado with a fork in a small bowl.
Toast the bread slices to your liking.
Spread the mashed avocado on the toast slices.
Once the eggs are done, add them on top of the avocado toast.
Optional: add diced cherry tomatoes or hot sauce/ pepper flakes on top of the eggs.
Serve and enjoy your breakfast or lunch.

Chapter 1: Breakfast

Greek yogurt with berries and honey

Ingredients:

1 cup plain Greek yogurt
1/2 cup mixed berries (such as strawberries, blueberries, and raspberries)
1 tbsp honey
Optional: 1 tbsp chopped nuts or granola

Directions:

In a small bowl, mix together the Greek yogurt and honey.
Add the mixed berries to the bowl and gently
stir to combine.
Optional: top with chopped nuts or granola
for added texture and flavor.
Serve and enjoy as breakfast or snack.
This recipe can be easily doubled or tripled if you want to feed more people or have leftovers. You could also experiment with different kind of berries or fruits.

Chapter 1: Breakfast

Peanut butter and banana smoothie

Ingredients:
1 banana
1/2 cup milk or any non-dairy milk
2 tbsp peanut butter
1 tbsp honey
4-5 ice cubes

Directions:
Peel and slice the banana.
In a blender, combine the banana, milk, peanut butter and honey.
Add the ice cubes and blend until smooth.
Serve and enjoy as breakfast or a snack.
Optional: You could add a scoop of protein powder, a tablespoon of cocoa powder, or a handful of spinach to boost the nutritional value of the smoothie.

This recipe can be easily doubled or tripled if you want to feed more people or have leftovers.

Chapter 1: Breakfast

Breakfast burrito with scrambled eggs and veggies

Ingredients:
2 large eggs
Salt and pepper, to taste
1 tsp butter or oil
1/4 cup diced vegetables (bell pepper, onion, tomatoes)
1/4 cup shredded cheese
2-3 flour tortillas

Directions:
Beat the eggs with a fork, season with salt and pepper.
In a skillet, melt the butter or oil. Add diced vegetables and cook for 2-3 minutes. Pour the beaten eggs into the skillet and cook until set. Stir in shredded cheese. Warm the tortillas, divide the egg mixture among them and roll to make burritos. Serve and enjoy as breakfast or brunch.
This version has the same instructions but with less detailed steps and less ingredients, you can still add bacon, ham or sausage if you want, or hot sauce or pepper flakes for a bit of heat.

Chapter 1: Breakfast

Omelet with mushrooms, peppers, and onions

Ingredients:
3 large eggs
Salt and pepper, to taste
1 tsp butter or oil
1/4 cup diced mushrooms
1/4 cup diced bell peppers
1/4 cup diced onions
Optional: shredded cheese, diced ham, or diced bacon.

Directions:
In a small bowl, beat the eggs with a fork or whisk. Season with salt and pepper.
In a skillet over medium heat, melt the butter or heat the oil.
Add the diced mushrooms, bell peppers, and onions to the skillet.
Cook for 2-3 minutes, until softened.
Pour the beaten eggs into the skillet and cook until set, about 2-3 minutes,
you can use a spatula to fold the omelet in half if you prefer.
Optional: top the omelet with shredded cheese or diced
ham or bacon before folding.
Serve and enjoy as breakfast or brunch.
This recipe can be easily doubled or tripled if you want to feed more people or have leftovers. And you could also add some hot sauce or pepper flakes
for a bit of heat.

Chapter 1: Breakfast

English muffin with ham and cheese

Ingredients:
1 English muffin
2 slices of ham
2 slices of cheese (cheddar or any cheese you prefer)
Butter or Margarine

Directions:
Preheat a skillet or griddle on medium heat.
Split the English muffin in half and spread butter or margarine on both sides.
Place the English muffin halves in the skillet or griddle, butter side down.
Add a slice of cheese on each half of the English muffin.
Add 2 slices of ham on one half of the English muffin,
make sure it covers the cheese.
Carefully close the sandwich with the other half of the English muffin.
Cook the sandwich for 2-3 minutes on each side or until the English
muffin is toasted and the cheese is melted.
Serve and enjoy as breakfast or brunch.
This recipe can be easily doubled or tripled if you want to feed more people or have leftovers. You could also add some extra ingredients like lettuce, tomato, or mayonnaise to make it more flavorful.

Chapter 1: Breakfast

Blueberry pancakes

Ingredients:

1 cup all-purpose flour
2 tbsp sugar
2 tsp baking powder
1/4 tsp salt
1 cup milk or any non-dairy milk
1 large egg
1 tsp vanilla extract
1/2 cup fresh or frozen blueberries
Butter or oil for cooking

Directions:

In a medium bowl, whisk together the flour, sugar, baking powder, and salt.
In a separate bowl, whisk together the milk, egg and vanilla extract.
Gradually add the wet ingredients to the dry ingredients,
stirring until just combined.
Gently fold in the blueberries.
Heat a skillet or griddle over medium-high heat and add butter or oil.
Using a ladle, pour batter onto the skillet or griddle.
Cook the pancakes for 2-3 minutes on each side or until golden brown.
Serve with butter and syrup and enjoy as breakfast or brunch.
This recipe can be easily doubled or tripled if you want to feed more people or have leftovers. You could also add some extra ingredients like chocolate chips, nuts, or other fruits to make it more flavorful.

Chapter 1: Breakfast

Quinoa bowls with eggs, veggies, and avocado

Ingredients:
1 cup cooked quinoa
1/2 bell pepper, diced
1/4 onion, diced
1/4 cup cherry tomatoes, halved
1/4 avocado, diced
2 eggs
Salt and pepper to taste
Olive oil for cooking

Directions:
In a pan, heat some olive oil over medium heat.
Add diced bell pepper and onion, and sauté until they are softened.
Add cherry tomatoes and sauté for an additional minute.
Make two wells in the pan, and crack an egg into each well.
Cook the eggs to your desired level of doneness.
In a bowl, combine the cooked quinoa, sautéed veggies, and diced avocado.
Top with the cooked eggs.
Season with salt and pepper to taste.
Enjoy!

Chapter 1: Breakfast

Breakfast sandwich with bacon, egg, and cheese

Ingredients:
2 slices of bread
2 slices of bacon
1 egg
1 slice of cheese
Salt and pepper to taste
Butter or margarine (optional)

Directions:
Cook the bacon in a pan over medium heat until crispy.
Remove from pan and set aside.
In the same pan, add butter or margarine if desired, and crack the egg into the pan.
Cook the egg to your desired level of doneness.
While the egg is cooking, toast the bread to your liking.
Assemble the sandwich by placing a slice of cheese on one slice of toast, add the cooked egg on top, followed by the bacon slices.
Place the other slice of toast on top and press down gently.
Cut the sandwich in half and serve.
Enjoy!

Chapter 1: Breakfast

Smoothie bowl with yogurt, berries, and granola

Ingredients:
1 cup of Greek yogurt
1/2 cup frozen berries (such as blueberries, raspberries, or a mix)
1/4 cup granola
1/4 cup milk or milk alternative
1 tsp honey (optional)

Directions:
Add yogurt, frozen berries, milk or milk alternative, and honey (if using) into a blender.
Blend on high speed until smooth and creamy.
Pour the smoothie into a bowl.
Top with granola.
Serve immediately and enjoy!
You can also add some toppings as you like like nuts, seeds, or drizzle some honey.
Enjoy!

Chapter 1: Breakfast

French toast with fresh fruit

Ingredients:

2 slices of bread
1 egg
1/4 cup milk
1 tsp sugar
1 tsp vanilla extract
1/4 tsp cinnamon (optional)
Fresh fruit of your choice (e.g. berries, banana, kiwi)
Butter or oil for cooking
Maple syrup for serving (optional)

Directions:

In a shallow dish, whisk together the egg, milk, sugar, vanilla extract, and cinnamon (if using)
Heat a pan over medium heat and add a small amount of butter or oil.
Dip the slices of bread into the egg mixture, ensuring that both sides are well coated.
Place the slices of bread onto the hot pan and cook until golden brown on each side, about 2-3 minutes per side.
Remove the French toast from the pan and place on a plate.
Top with fresh fruit of your choice and serve with maple syrup (if desired).
Enjoy!

Chapter 1: Breakfast

Breakfast potatoes with eggs and bacon

Ingredients:
1 medium-sized potato, peeled and diced
2 slices of bacon
2 eggs
Salt and pepper to taste
Butter or oil for cooking

Directions:
In a pan, cook the bacon until crispy. Remove from the pan and set aside.
In the same pan, add some butter or oil and sauté the diced potatoes until they are cooked through and golden brown. Season with salt and pepper to taste.
Make two wells in the pan, and crack an egg into each well.
Cook the eggs to your desired level of doneness.
Crumble the cooked bacon and add it to the pan with the potatoes and eggs.
Toss everything together and cook for an additional minute.
Serve the potatoes, eggs, and bacon in a plate, and enjoy your breakfast.
You can also season with some herbs or spices as you like.
Enjoy!

Chapter 1: Breakfast

Yogurt parfait with granola and fruit

Ingredients:
1 cup of Greek yogurt
1/4 cup of granola
1/4 cup of fresh fruit of your choice (e.g. berries, banana, kiwi)
1 tsp honey (optional)

Directions:
In a tall glass or jar, add a layer of Greek yogurt on the bottom.
Add a layer of granola on top of the yogurt.
Add a layer of fresh fruit on top of the granola.
Repeat the layers until you reach the top of the glass or jar.
Drizzle honey on top if desired.
Serve and enjoy!
You can also use different types of yogurt or granola, or add any other toppings such as nuts, seeds, or drizzle some honey, chocolate chips, or peanut butter.
Enjoy!

Chapter 1: Breakfast

Breakfast hash with sweet potatoes, bacon, and eggs

Ingredients:
1 sweet potato, peeled and diced
2 slices of bacon
2 eggs
Salt and pepper to taste
Butter or oil for cooking

Directions:
In a pan, cook the bacon until crispy. Remove from the pan and set aside.
In the same pan, add some butter or oil and sauté the diced sweet potatoes until they are cooked through and golden brown. Season with salt and pepper to taste.
Make two wells in the pan, and crack an egg into each well.
Cook the eggs to your desired level of doneness.
Crumble the cooked bacon and add it to the pan with the sweet potatoes and eggs.
Toss everything together and cook for an additional minute.
Serve the sweet potato hash, eggs, and bacon in a plate, and enjoy your breakfast.
You can also season with some herbs or spices as you like.
Enjoy!

Chapter 1: Breakfast

Bagel with tomato, avocado and bacon

Ingredients:
1 bagel, split and toasted
1/2 tomato, sliced
1/2 avocado, mashed
2 slices of bacon, cooked and crumbled
Mayo (if you like)

Directions:
Toast the bagel until it is golden brown and crispy.
Spread the mashed avocado on one half of the toasted bagel.
Place the tomato slices on top of the avocado.
Sprinkle the crumbled bacon over the tomato slices.
Top with the other half of the bagel and enjoy!
Optional: you can also add some salt, pepper and olive oil to taste.

Chapter 1: Breakfast

Breakfast pizza with sausage, egg, and cheese

Ingredients:
1 pre-made pizza crust or homemade pizza dough
1/4 cup of cooked breakfast sausage
2 eggs
1/4 cup of shredded cheese (cheddar, mozzarella or any cheese you prefer)
Salt and pepper to taste
Olive oil or butter for cooking

Directions:
Preheat your oven to 425°F (220°C) or according to the package instructions if you are using a pre-made pizza crust.
Roll out the dough or press it out onto a greased baking sheet or pizza pan.
Spread the cooked breakfast sausage over the pizza crust.
Crack the eggs over the sausage and top with shredded cheese.
Season with salt and pepper to taste.
Bake for 10-15 minutes or until the crust is golden brown and the cheese is melted.
Remove from the oven and let it cool for a couple of minutes before slicing.
Serve and enjoy!
You can also add other toppings of your choice like bell pepper, mushrooms, onion, etc.

Chapter 1: Breakfast

Chia seed pudding with almond milk and fruit

Ingredients:
1/4 cup chia seeds
1 cup unsweetened almond milk
1/2 tsp vanilla extract
1 tablespoon honey or other sweeteners of your choice(optional)
1/2 cup fresh fruit of your choice (e.g. berries, banana, kiwi)

Directions:
In a medium bowl, mix together chia seeds, almond milk,
vanilla extract, and honey (if using).
Cover the bowl with plastic wrap and refrigerate overnight or for at least 4 hours, or until the chia seeds have thickened and the pudding has a jelly-like consistency.
Once the pudding has set, add fresh fruit on top and serve.
You can also add other toppings of your choice like nuts, seeds, or
drizzle some honey or chocolate chips.
This recipe is very versatile, you can use any type of milk or sweeteners of your choice, and also add any type of fruits or toppings you like.
Enjoy!

Chapter 1: Breakfast

Oatmeal with nuts, seeds, and dried fruit

Ingredients:
1/2 cup rolled oats
1 cup water or milk
1/4 cup mixed nuts (such as almonds, walnuts, or pecans)
1/4 cup mixed seeds (such as pumpkin, sunflower or flax seeds)
1/4 cup dried fruit (such as raisins, cranberries, or apricots)
1 tbsp honey or maple syrup (optional)

Directions:
In a small saucepan, bring the water or milk to a boil.
Stir in the rolled oats and reduce heat to low.
Cook for 2-3 minutes, or until the oats have absorbed the liquid and are tender.
Remove from heat and stir in the mixed nuts, seeds, and dried fruit.
Sweeten with honey or maple syrup (if desired)
Serve and enjoy!
You can also add some toppings as you like like a dollop of peanut butter or yogurt.

Chapter 1: Breakfast

Breakfast wrap with sausage, egg, and cheese.

Ingredients:
1 large flour tortilla
1/4 cup of cooked breakfast sausage
2 eggs
1/4 cup of shredded cheese (cheddar, mozzarella or any cheese you prefer)
Salt and pepper to taste
Butter or oil for cooking

Directions:
Heat a skillet over medium heat and add a small amount of butter or oil.
Crack the eggs into the skillet and season with salt and pepper.
Cook to your desired doneness.
Remove the eggs from the skillet and set aside.
In the same skillet, add the cooked breakfast sausage and cook for 1-2 minutes.
Place the flour tortilla on a plate and add the cooked eggs,
sausage and shredded cheese in the center.
Fold the bottom of the tortilla up, then fold in the sides and roll up tightly.
Cut in half and serve.
Enjoy your breakfast wrap!
You can add some veggies like spinach, bell pepper, or onion to make it more colorful and nutritious.

Chapter 2: Lunch

Grilled chicken Caesar salad

Ingredients:
1 boneless, skinless chicken breast
Salt and pepper to taste
2 tbsp of Caesar dressing
1/2 head of Romaine lettuce, washed and chopped
2 tbsp of croutons
2 tbsp of grated Parmesan cheese

Directions:
Preheat your grill or grill pan over medium-high heat.
Season the chicken breast with salt and pepper.
Grill the chicken for 4-5 minutes per side, or until cooked through.
Let the chicken cool slightly, then slice it into thin strips.
In a medium bowl, combine the Romaine lettuce, croutons, and Parmesan cheese.
Add the grilled chicken strips to the bowl and toss with Caesar dressing.
Serve and enjoy!
You can also add other toppings of your choice like tomatoes, cucumbers, or bacon.

Chapter 2: Lunch

Turkey and cheese wrap with avocado and tomato

Ingredients:
1 large flour tortilla
4-6 oz of sliced turkey breast
2-3 slices of cheese (cheddar, swiss or any cheese you prefer)
1/4 of an avocado, mashed
2-3 cherry tomatoes, sliced
Salt and pepper to taste
Butter or mayonnaise (optional)

Directions:
Spread butter or mayonnaise on the flour tortilla (if using)
Place the turkey slices in the center of the tortilla, followed by the cheese, mashed avocado, and sliced tomatoes.
Season with salt and pepper to taste.
Fold the bottom of the tortilla up, then fold in the sides and roll up tightly.
Cut in half and serve.
Enjoy your wrap!
You can add some greens like lettuce or spinach for added color and nutrition.

Chapter 2: Lunch

Tuna salad sandwich

Ingredients:

1 can of tuna, drained
2 tbsp of mayonnaise
1/4 cup of diced celery
1/4 cup of diced onion
1 tbsp of lemon juice
Salt and pepper to taste
2 slices of bread
Lettuce or spinach leaves (optional)
Tomato slices (optional)

Directions:

In a medium bowl, mix together the tuna, mayonnaise, celery, onion, and lemon juice.
Season with salt and pepper to taste.
Toast the bread to your liking.
Spread the tuna salad on one slice of toast, and top with lettuce or spinach leaves, and tomato slices if desired.
Place the other slice of toast on top and press down gently.
Cut the sandwich in half and serve.
Enjoy your sandwich!
You can also add other ingredients like pickles, hard-boiled eggs, or avocado to make it more flavorful and nutritious.

Chapter 2: Lunch

Black bean and sweet potato burrito

Ingredients:

1 large flour tortilla
1/2 cup of cooked and mashed sweet potato
1/2 cup of cooked black beans
1/4 cup of diced red bell pepper
1/4 cup of diced onion
1/4 cup of shredded cheese (cheddar, mozzarella or any cheese you prefer)
Salt and pepper to taste
1/4 cup of salsa or hot sauce (optional)

Directions:

Preheat a skillet over medium heat and add the diced red bell pepper and onion. Cook until they are softened.
Add the cooked and mashed sweet potato and black beans to the skillet and cook for an additional 2-3 minutes.
Season with salt and pepper to taste.
Place the flour tortilla on a plate, and add the sweet potato and black bean mixture in the center.
Top with shredded cheese and salsa or hot sauce if desired.
Fold the bottom of the tortilla up, then fold in the sides and roll up tightly.
Heat the skillet again and cook the burrito for 1-2 minutes on each side, or until it is crispy and golden brown.
Cut the burrito in half and serve.
You can also add other toppings like avocado, sour cream, or cilantro if you wish.
Enjoy!

Chapter 2: Lunch

Greek salad with grilled chicken

Ingredients:

1 boneless, skinless chicken breast
Salt and pepper to taste
1/4 cup of olive oil
2 tbsp of lemon juice
1/4 tsp of dried oregano
1/4 of a red onion, sliced
1/2 of a cucumber, sliced
1/2 cup of cherry tomatoes, halved
1/4 cup of Kalamata olives
1/4 cup of crumbled feta cheese

Directions:

Preheat your grill or grill pan over medium-high heat.
Season the chicken breast with salt and pepper.
Grill the chicken for 4-5 minutes per side, or until cooked through.
Let the chicken cool slightly, then slice it into thin strips.
In a large bowl, whisk together the olive oil, lemon juice, and dried oregano.
Add the red onion, cucumber, cherry tomatoes, olives,
and chicken to the bowl and toss to combine.
Top with crumbled feta cheese.
Serve and enjoy!
You can also add some greens like lettuce or spinach for added color and nutrition.

Chapter 2: Lunch

Quinoa and veggie stir-fry

Ingredients:
1/2 cup of cooked quinoa
1/2 cup of mixed vegetables (such as bell peppers, mushrooms, carrots, and broccoli)
1 tbsp of oil (such as vegetable or olive oil)
1 clove of garlic, minced
1/4 cup of soy sauce
1 tsp of honey or brown sugar
Salt and pepper to taste
Sesame seeds and green onions for garnish (optional)

Directions:
Heat a wok or large pan over high heat and add the oil.
Add the garlic and cook for 30 seconds until fragrant.
Add the mixed vegetables and stir-fry for 3-4 minutes until they are tender.
Add the cooked quinoa, soy sauce, and honey or brown sugar to the pan and stir-fry for an additional 2-3 minutes.
Season with salt and pepper to taste.
Garnish with sesame seeds and green onions if desired.
Serve and enjoy!
You can also add other ingredients like tofu, chicken, or shrimp to make it more flavorful and nutritious.

Chapter 2: Lunch

Turkey burger with sweet potato fries

Ingredients:
1 lb ground turkey
1/4 cup diced onion
1/4 cup diced bell pepper
1 tsp salt
1 tsp pepper
1 tsp of your favorite herbs or spices
1 large sweet potato, cut into fries
Oil for frying

Directions:
Mix together ground turkey, onion, bell pepper, salt, pepper, and herbs/spices.
Form into a patty.
Grill or pan-fry the patty until cooked through.
Deep fry or oven-bake sweet potato fries until crispy.
Serve the turkey burger with the sweet potato fries and enjoy.
You can also add toppings as you like like cheese, lettuce, tomato, onion, etc.
Enjoy!

Chapter 2: Lunch

Spinach and feta omelet

Ingredients:
2 large eggs
Salt and pepper, to taste
1 tsp butter or oil
1/4 cup fresh spinach leaves
2 tbsp crumbled feta cheese

Directions:
In a small bowl, beat the eggs with a fork or whisk. Season with salt and pepper.
In a skillet over medium heat, melt the butter or heat the oil.
Add the spinach leaves to skillet and cook
until they begin to wilt about 1-2 minutes.
Pour the beaten eggs into the skillet and stir gently with a spatula until the eggs are cooked through, about 2-3 minutes.
Remove the skillet from the heat and sprinkle feta cheese on top of the eggs.
Fold the omelet in half, or use a spatula to fold it.
Serve and enjoy as breakfast or brunch.
Optional: You could add diced tomatoes, onions or mushrooms to the skillet with the spinach before adding the eggs. And you could also add some
hot sauce or pepper flakes for a bit of heat.

Broccoli and cheddar soup

Ingredients:
1 tbsp butter or oil
1/4 cup diced onions
1 clove of garlic, minced
1 cup chopped broccoli florets
1 cup chicken or vegetable broth
1 cup whole milk or heavy cream
1 cup shredded cheddar cheese
Salt and pepper, to taste

Directions:
In a pot or a large saucepan, melt the butter or heat the oil over medium heat.
Add diced onions and minced garlic, cook until softened, about 2-3 minutes.
Add the broccoli florets and cook for another 2-3 minutes.
Pour in the broth and bring to a simmer.
Reduce heat to low and cover the pot, let the broccoli cook until tender, about 10-15 minutes.
Remove the pot from the heat and use an immersion blender or transfer the soup to a blender and puree until smooth.
Return the pot to the heat and stir in the milk or cream and shredded cheese.
Stir until the cheese is melted and the soup is heated through.
Season with salt and pepper to taste.
Serve and enjoy as a main course or as a side dish.

Chapter 2: Lunch

Chicken and vegetable curry

Ingredients:
1 tbsp oil
1 small onion, diced
1 tsp curry powder
1/4 tsp salt
1 boneless, skinless chicken breast, diced
1 cup mixed diced vegetables (carrots, potatoes, bell peppers, tomatoes)
1 cup coconut milk

Directions:
In a large skillet or pot over medium heat, heat the oil.
Add onion and sauté for 2-3 minutes.
Add curry powder, salt, chicken and mixed vegetables, sauté for 5 minutes or until chicken is cooked through.
Pour in coconut milk, bring to a simmer, cover and simmer for 15-20 minutes or until vegetables are tender.
Serve and enjoy the curry as a main course.
This version has the same instructions but with less detailed steps and less ingredients. You could add some spices like cumin, turmeric, ginger, black pepper to enhance the flavor.

Chapter 2: Lunch

Turkey chili with avocado

Ingredients:

1 lb ground turkey
1 can diced tomatoes
1 can kidney beans
1 small onion, diced
1 red bell pepper, diced
2 cloves garlic, minced
1 tsp chili powder
Salt and pepper to taste
1 avocado, diced

Directions:

Cook turkey in a pot until browned.
Add diced tomatoes, kidney beans, onion, red bell pepper, garlic, chili powder, salt and pepper to the pot.
Simmer for 25-30 minutes or until vegetables are tender.
Serve chili in bowls, top with diced avocado.
. You could add some extra spices or other ingredients as you desired.

Chapter 2: Lunch
Grilled chicken and veggie kabobs

Ingredients:
1 lb boneless, skinless chicken breasts, cut into 1-inch cubes
1 red bell pepper, cut into 1-inch squares
1 yellow bell pepper, cut into 1-inch squares
1 red onion, cut into 1-inch squares
1 zucchini, cut into 1-inch slices
1/2 cup olive oil
2 cloves garlic, minced
1 tsp dried oregano & dried thyme
Salt and pepper to taste
Wooden skewers, soaked in water for at least 30 minutes

Directions:
In a large bowl, whisk together the olive oil, garlic, oregano, thyme, salt, and pepper.
Add the chicken, peppers, onion, and zucchini to the bowl and toss to coat with the marinade.
Cover the bowl with plastic wrap and refrigerate for at least 1 hour, or up to 4 hours.
Preheat grill to medium-high heat.
Thread the chicken and vegetables onto the skewers, alternating between the different ingredients.
Grill the kabobs for 12-15 minutes, turning occasionally, until the chicken is cooked through and the vegetables are slightly charred.

Chapter 2: Lunch

Turkey meatloaf with roasted vegetables

Ingredients:
1 lb ground turkey
1 egg
1/4 cup breadcrumbs
1/4 cup diced onions
1 clove of garlic, minced
1 tsp dried thyme
Salt and pepper to taste
1 cup mixed diced vegetables (carrots, potatoes, bell peppers, tomatoes)

Directions:
Preheat oven to 375F.
In a large bowl, combine ground turkey, egg, breadcrumbs, onion, garlic, thyme, salt and pepper. Mix until well combined.
Shape the mixture into a loaf and place it in a baking dish.
Place the diced vegetables around the meatloaf.
Bake for 45-50 minutes or until the meatloaf is cooked through and the vegetables are tender.
You could add some more spices or herbs if you desire to enhance the flavor.

Chapter 2: Lunch

BBQ Chicken sandwich

Ingredients:

1 boneless, skinless chicken breast
Salt and pepper, to taste
1 tablespoon olive oil
1 teaspoon BBQ seasoning (store-bought or homemade)
2 slices of bread (your choice)
1-2 slices of cheese (optional)
Lettuce and tomato, for topping (optional)
BBQ sauce, for serving (optional)

Directions:

Preheat a grill or grill pan to medium-high heat.
Season the chicken breast with salt, pepper, olive oil and BBQ seasoning.
Grill the chicken breast for 4-5 minutes per side or until fully cooked.
Shred the chicken
Toast the bread or buns slices on the grill or in a toaster.
Assemble the sandwich by placing the shredded chicken breast on one slice of bread and topping it with cheese, lettuce and tomato, if desired.
Spread BBQ sauce on the other slice of bread and place it on top of the sandwich to complete it.
Serve and enjoy!

Chapter 2: Lunch

Turkey and cheese quesadilla

Ingredients:
2 flour tortillas
1/4 cup shredded cheese (cheddar, Monterey jack, or any cheese you prefer)
1/4 cup shredded cooked turkey
1/4 cup diced bell peppers
1/4 cup diced onions
Salt and pepper to taste
1 tbsp oil or butter

Directions:
Preheat a skillet or griddle over medium-high heat.
On one tortilla, add shredded cheese, shredded turkey, diced bell peppers, diced onions, salt and pepper.
Place the other tortilla on top of the ingredients to make a sandwich.
Add oil or butter to the skillet or griddle.
Place the quesadilla in the skillet or griddle and cook for 2-3 minutes on each side or until golden brown and the cheese is melted.
Cut the quesadilla into wedges and serve with sour cream or guacamole as dipping sauce.
You could also add some extra ingredients like diced tomatoes, jalapenos, or black beans to make it more flavorful.

Chapter 2: Lunch

Grilled chicken and vegetable pasta

Ingredients:
8 oz of pasta (spaghetti, fettuccine, or any pasta you prefer)
1 boneless, skinless chicken breast, cut into 1-inch cubes
1 red bell pepper, cut into 1-inch squares
1 yellow bell pepper, cut into 1-inch squares
1 red onion, cut into 1-inch squares
1 zucchini, cut into 1-inch slices
2 cloves of garlic, minced
2 tbsp olive oil
1 tsp dried oregano & 1 tsp dried basil
Salt and pepper to taste
1/4 cup grated parmesan cheese

Directions:
Cook the pasta according to package instructions, drain, and set aside.
In a large bowl, mix together the chicken, peppers, onion, zucchini, garlic, olive oil, oregano, basil, salt, and pepper.
Heat a grill or grill pan over medium-high heat.
Grill the chicken and vegetables for 8-10 minutes or until cooked through.
In a large bowl, toss the pasta with the grilled chicken and vegetables.
Serve and top with grated parmesan cheese and enjoy.
You could also add some other vegetables like mushrooms, cherry tomatoes, or use different types of meat such as pork or beef.

Chapter 2: Lunch

Turkey and avocado lettuce cups

Ingredients:
8-12 lettuce leaves (butter, iceburg or romaine lettuce)
1/2 lb cooked and shredded turkey
1 ripe avocado, diced
1/4 cup diced red onion
1/4 cup diced tomato
2 tbsp chopped cilantro
2 tbsp lime juice
1 tbsp olive oil
Salt and pepper to taste

Directions:
In a medium bowl, mix together the turkey, avocado, red onion, tomato, cilantro, lime juice, olive oil, salt and pepper.
Carefully remove the lettuce leaves from the head of lettuce, making sure they stay in their natural cup shape.
Spoon the turkey mixture into each lettuce cup.
Serve and enjoy as a main course or appetizer.
You could also add some other ingredients like diced jalapenos, or cheese, or use different types of meat such as chicken or pork, or use a different type of avocado.

Chapter 2: Lunch

Turkey and cheese melt with tomato soup

Ingredients:
2 slices of bread (white, whole wheat, or any bread you prefer)
2 slices of turkey
2 slices of cheese (cheddar, Swiss, or any cheese you prefer)
2 tbsp butter
1 can of tomato soup
Salt and pepper to taste

Directions:
Preheat a skillet or griddle over medium heat.
Butter one side of each slice of bread.
Place the bread, butter side down, on the skillet or griddle.
Add a slice of cheese and a slice of turkey on top of one of the bread slices.
Close the sandwich by placing the other bread slice on top, butter side up.
Cook for 2-3 minutes on each side or until golden brown and the cheese is melted.
Heat the tomato soup on the stove or in the microwave.
Add salt and pepper to taste.
Serve the sandwich with the tomato soup and enjoy.
You could also add some other ingredients like avocado, bacon, or lettuce, or use different types of cheese or bread

Chapter 2: Lunch

Turkey and veggie stir fry with brown rice

Ingredients:

1/2 cup uncooked brown rice
1 lb cooked and shredded turkey
1 red bell pepper, sliced
1 yellow bell pepper, sliced
1 onion, sliced
1 cup sliced mushrooms
2 cloves of garlic, minced
2 tbsp soy sauce
1 tbsp vegetable oil
Salt and pepper to taste
Fresh cilantro or green onions, chopped (optional)

Directions:

Cook the rice according to package instructions. Once it's cooked, set it aside.
In a large skillet or wok, heat the oil over medium-high heat.
Add the turkey, peppers, onion, mushrooms, and garlic.
Cook for 4-5 minutes or until the vegetables are tender.
Add soy sauce, salt, and pepper to taste.
Cook for an additional 1-2 minutes.
Serve the stir fry over the cooked brown rice.
Garnish with fresh cilantro or green onions, if desired.

Chapter 2: Lunch

Turkey and cheese panini with pesto

Ingredients:
2 slices of bread (ciabatta, focaccia, or any bread you prefer)
2 slices of turkey
2 slices of cheese (mozzarella, provolone, or any cheese you prefer)
2 tbsp pesto sauce
2 tbsp butter
Salt and pepper to taste

Directions:
Preheat a panini press or a large skillet over medium-high heat.
Spread the pesto sauce on one side of each slice of bread.
Place the turkey and cheese on one slice of bread
and close the sandwich with the other slice of bread.
Spread butter on the outside of the sandwich.
Place the sandwich on the panini press or in the skillet.
Cook for 3-4 minutes on each side or until the bread is
toasted and the cheese is melted.
Cut the sandwich in half and serve, adding salt and pepper to taste if desired.
You could also add some other ingredients like bacon, tomato, or avocado to make
it more flavorful.

Chapter 3: Appetizers

Deviled Eggs

Ingredients:
6 eggs
2 tbsp mayonnaise
1 tsp Dijon mustard
1 tsp white vinegar
Salt and pepper to taste
Paprika for garnish

Directions:
Place the eggs in a medium saucepan and add enough cold water to cover the eggs by 1 inch.
Place the saucepan over high heat and bring the water to a boil. Once the water boils, cover the saucepan and remove it from the heat.
Let the eggs sit in the hot water for 10-12 minutes.
Drain the hot water and place the eggs in a bowl of ice water.
Let sit for 5-10 minutes.
Peel the eggs and cut them in half lengthwise.
Remove the yolks and place them in a small bowl.
Mash the yolks with a fork or a pastry cutter.
Add the mayonnaise, mustard, white vinegar, salt, and pepper to the mashed yolks and mix well.
Spoon the mixture into the egg white halves.
Sprinkle with paprika for garnish.
You could also add some other ingredients like diced pickles, chopped green onions, or hot sauce to make it more flavorful.

Chapter 3: Appetizers

Guacamole and Chips

Ingredients:
2 ripe avocados
1 lime, juiced
1/4 cup diced tomatoes
1/4 cup diced onions
2 tbsp chopped cilantro
Salt and pepper to taste
Tortilla chips

Directions:
Cut the avocados in half and remove the pit.
Scoop the avocado flesh into a medium bowl.
Mash the avocado with a fork or a potato masher.
Add the lime juice, diced tomatoes, diced onions, cilantro, salt, and pepper to the mashed avocado and mix well.
Serve the guacamole with tortilla chips as an appetizer or snack.
This recipe can be easily doubled or tripled if you want to feed more people or have leftovers. You could also add some other ingredients like diced jalapenos, or garlic, or add some heat with some hot sauce or pepper flakes.

Chapter 3: Appetizers

Caprese Salad Skewers

Ingredients:
1 pint of cherry tomatoes
8 oz fresh mozzarella balls
Fresh basil leaves
2 tbsp olive oil
1 tbsp balsamic vinegar
Salt and pepper to taste
Skewers (if using wooden skewers, soak them in water for at least 30 minutes)

Directions:
Alternate cherry tomatoes, fresh mozzarella balls,
and fresh basil leaves on skewers.
In a small bowl, mix together the olive oil, balsamic vinegar, salt and pepper.
Brush the skewers with the oil and vinegar mixture.
Grill or broil the skewers for 2-3 minutes on each side,
or until the mozzarella is slightly melted.
Serve and enjoy as an appetizer or a side dish.
This recipe can be easily doubled or tripled if you want to feed more people or have leftovers. You could also add some other ingredients like fresh mushrooms, or use different types of cheese or tomatoes.

Chapter 3: Appetizers

Cheesy Garlic Bread

Ingredients:
1 baguette or 1-2 loaves of Italian bread
1/4 cup butter, softened
3 cloves of garlic, minced
1/4 cup grated parmesan cheese
Salt and pepper to taste

Directions:
Preheat the oven to 350°F (175°C).
Cut the bread into slices, about 1/2 inch thick.
In a small bowl, mix together the butter, minced garlic, salt, and pepper.
Spread the butter mixture on one side of each slice of bread.
Place the bread slices on a baking sheet.
Sprinkle grated cheese over the bread slices.
Bake for about 10-15 minutes or until the bread is golden brown and the cheese is melted.
Serve and enjoy as an appetizer or a side dish.
This recipe can be easily doubled or tripled if you want to feed more people or have leftovers. You could also add some other ingredients like herbs, or use different types of cheese.

Chapter 3: Appetizers

Baked Brie

Ingredients:
1 wheel of brie cheese
1 sheet of puff pastry, thawed
1 egg, beaten

Directions:
Preheat the oven to 400°F (200°C).
Roll out the puff pastry sheet on a lightly floured surface to a thickness of 1/8 inch.
Place the wheel of brie in the center of the puff pastry.
Bring the edges of the puff pastry up around the brie,
pinching the seams together to seal.
Brush the puff pastry with beaten egg.
Place the brie on a baking sheet lined with parchment paper.
Bake for about 15-20 minutes or until the puff pastry is golden brown and puffed.
Serve the brie with crackers or bread and enjoy as an appetizer or a light meal.
This recipe can be easily doubled or tripled if you want to feed more people or have leftovers. You could also add some other ingredients
like herbs, or use different types of cheese.

Chapter 3: Appetizers

Cream Cheese Stuffed Jalapenos

Ingredients:
8 jalapeno peppers
4 oz cream cheese, softened
1/4 cup shredded cheddar cheese
Salt and pepper to taste

Directions:
Preheat the oven to 375°F (190°C).
Cut the jalapeno peppers in half lengthwise and
remove the seeds and membranes.
In a small bowl, mix together the cream cheese,
shredded cheddar cheese, salt, and pepper.
Spoon the mixture into the jalapeno pepper halves.
Place the stuffed jalapenos on a baking sheet lined with parchment paper.
Bake for about 10-15 minutes or until the cheese is melted and
the jalapenos are slightly tender.
Serve and enjoy as an appetizer or a side dish.
This recipe can be easily doubled or tripled if you want to feed more people or
have leftovers. You could also add some other ingredients
like diced bacon, or use different types of cheese.

Chapter 3: Appetizers

Stuffed Mushrooms

Ingredients:
8-10 large mushrooms
2 tbsp breadcrumbs
2 tbsp grated parmesan cheese
1 tbsp chopped fresh parsley
1 clove of garlic, minced
Salt and pepper to taste
Olive oil for brushing

Directions:
Preheat the oven to 375°F (190°C).
Clean the mushrooms by gently wiping them with a damp cloth.
Remove the stems and chop them finely.
In a small bowl, mix together the breadcrumbs, parmesan cheese, parsley, garlic, salt, pepper, and the chopped mushroom stems.
Brush the mushroom caps with a little olive oil.
Stuff the mushroom caps with the breadcrumb mixture.
Place the mushrooms on a baking sheet lined with parchment paper.
Bake for about 15-20 minutes or until the mushrooms are tender and the filling is golden brown.
Serve and enjoy as an appetizer or a side dish.
This recipe can be easily doubled or tripled if you want to feed more people or have leftovers. You could also add some other ingredients like diced bacon or sausage, or use different types of cheese.

Chapter 3: Appetizers

Mini Meatballs

Ingredients:
1 pound ground beef or pork
1/4 cup breadcrumbs
1/4 cup grated Parmesan cheese
1 egg
1 clove garlic, minced
1 teaspoon salt
1/4 teaspoon black pepper
1 tablespoon olive oil

Directions:
In a large bowl, combine the ground beef or pork, breadcrumbs, Parmesan cheese, egg, garlic, salt, and pepper.
Mix well.
Roll the mixture into small meatballs, about the size of a golf ball.
Heat the olive oil in a large skillet over medium heat.
Add the meatballs to the skillet and cook for about 8-10 minutes, or until browned on all sides and cooked through.
Serve the meatballs with your favorite sauce or as a topping on a sandwich or pasta dish.
Note: You can make a big batch of the meatballs and freeze them for future use.

Chapter 3: Appetizers

Spinach and Feta Spanakopita

Ingredients:
1/2 onion, finely chopped
2 cloves garlic, minced
1 (10 oz) package frozen spinach, thawed and squeezed dry
1/4 cup crumbled feta cheese
2 tablespoons chopped fresh dill
2 tablespoons chopped fresh parsley
1/4 teaspoon ground black pepper
1/4 cup butter, melted
1/4 cup all-purpose flour
1 cup milk
1 egg, lightly beaten
1/2 package of phyllo pastry (about 8-10 sheets)

Directions:
Preheat the oven to 350°F (180°C).
In a skillet, cook onion and garlic until softened.
Mix in spinach, feta, dill, parsley, and pepper.
In the same skillet, melt butter and stir in flour. Gradually stir in
milk and cook until thickened. Remove from heat and stir in beaten egg.
Place 4 sheets of phyllo in a 9-inch (23 cm) square baking dish, brushing each one
with melted butter. Spread spinach mixture over phyllo, top with
4 more sheets of phyllo, brushing each one with butter.
Cut into squares or triangles and bake for 25-30 minutes or until golden brown.
Serve warm.

Chapter 3: Appetizers

Prosciutto Wrapped Melon

Ingredients:
1 ripe cantaloupe or honeydew melon
8 thin slices of prosciutto

Directions:
Cut the melon in half and scoop out the seeds. Cut the melon into 8 wedges. Take one slice of prosciutto and wrap it around the center of one melon wedge, securing the prosciutto with a toothpick if necessary. Repeat with the remaining slices of prosciutto and melon wedges.
Serve chilled as a starter or a light snack.
Note: You can also add some fresh mint leaves or a drizzle of balsamic glaze for extra flavor.

Enjoy!

Chapter 3: Appetizers

Cucumber and Dill Tea Sandwiches

Ingredients:
4 slices white bread
4 tablespoons cream cheese, softened
1/4 cup finely chopped cucumber
1 tablespoon chopped fresh dill
Salt and pepper, to taste

Directions:
Cut the crusts off the bread and flatten the slices with a rolling pin.
In a small bowl, mix together the cream cheese, cucumber, dill, salt, and pepper.
Spread the mixture evenly onto two slices of bread.
Top with the remaining two slices of bread to make sandwiches.
Cut the sandwiches into triangles or desired shape.
Serve chilled as a starter or a light snack.
Note: You can also add a sprinkle of smoked paprika or a squeeze of lemon juice to the cream cheese mixture for extra flavor.
Enjoy!

Chapter 3: Appetizers
Fried Green Beans

Ingredients:
1/2 pound fresh green beans, trimmed
1/2 cup all-purpose flour
1/2 teaspoon salt
1/4 teaspoon black pepper
1 egg & 1/4 cup milk
1/2 cup breadcrumbs
Vegetable oil for frying

Directions:
In a large pot of boiling water, blanch the green beans for about 2-3 minutes or until tender but still crispy. Drain and pat dry.
In a shallow dish, mix together the flour, salt, and pepper.
In another shallow dish, beat the egg and milk together.
Place the breadcrumbs in a third shallow dish.
Dip the green beans in the flour mixture, then the egg mixture, and then the breadcrumbs, pressing the breadcrumbs onto the beans to adhere.
Heat the vegetable oil in a large skillet over medium-high heat.
Once the oil is hot, add the breaded green beans and cook for 2-3 minutes on each side or until golden brown.
Remove the green beans from the skillet and drain on a paper towel.
Serve warm as a side dish or appetizer.
Note: You can also add some garlic powder, paprika or other spices to the flour mixture for extra flavor.
Enjoy!

Chapter 3: Appetizers

Buffalo Chicken Dip

Ingredients:
2 boneless, skinless chicken breasts
1/4 cup buffalo wing sauce
8 oz cream cheese, softened
1/4 cup sour cream
1/4 cup ranch dressing
1/4 cup crumbled blue cheese
1/4 cup shredded cheddar cheese
Salt and pepper to taste

Directions:
Preheat the oven to 350°F (175°C).
Cook the chicken breasts in a skillet over medium-high heat until fully cooked, about 8-10 minutes per side. Once cooked, shred the chicken with two forks or chop it into small pieces.
In a mixing bowl, combine the shredded chicken, buffalo wing sauce, cream cheese, sour cream, ranch dressing, blue cheese, cheddar cheese, salt, and pepper.
Transfer the mixture to a baking dish.
Bake for 20-25 minutes or until the cheese is melted and bubbly.
Serve the dip warm with crackers, celery sticks or veggies for dipping.
Note: You can also make it in a slow cooker, just put all ingredients in the slow cooker and cook on low for 2 hours.

Chapter 3: Appetizers

Shrimp Cocktail

Ingredients:
1 lb cooked shrimp, peeled and deveined
1/4 cup ketchup
2 tbsp prepared horseradish
1 tbsp lemon juice
1 tsp Worcestershire sauce
Salt and pepper to taste
Lemon wedges and parsley for garnish

Directions:
Rinse the shrimp and pat them dry.
In a mixing bowl, combine the ketchup, horseradish, lemon juice, Worcestershire sauce, salt, and pepper. Mix well.
Add the shrimp to the bowl and toss until they are well coated.
Cover and refrigerate for at least 30 minutes to allow the flavors to meld.
Arrange the shrimp on a platter, and garnish with lemon wedges and parsley.
Serve chilled with the cocktail sauce.

Chapter 3: Appetizers

Smoked Salmon and Cream Cheese

Ingredients:
4 oz cream cheese, at room temperature
2 tbsp chopped fresh dill
2 tbsp chopped fresh chives
Salt and pepper to taste
8 oz smoked salmon, thinly sliced
Crackers or bagel chips for serving

Directions:
In a mixing bowl, combine the cream cheese, dill, chives, salt, and pepper. Mix well.
Spread the cream cheese mixture on a plate or platter.
Arrange the smoked salmon on top of the cream cheese.
Serve with crackers or bagel chips.
Enjoy your appetizer!
Note: You can add or substitute any herbs or spices to your taste preference. Also, you can use any type of bread or crackers you like to serve it with.

Chapter 3: Appetizers

Pesto and Ricotta Crostini

Ingredients:
1 french baguette, sliced
1/4 cup pesto
1/4 cup ricotta cheese
Salt and pepper to taste
Fresh basil or parsley for garnish (optional)

Directions:
Preheat your oven to 350°F (175°C) and line a baking sheet with parchment paper.
Arrange the baguette slices on the baking sheet.
Spread the pesto over each slice of bread, then top
each with a dollop of ricotta cheese.
Sprinkle with a pinch of salt and pepper
Bake for 12-15 minutes or until the bread is golden
brown and the cheese is melted.
Remove from the oven and let it cool for a few minutes.
Garnish with fresh basil or parsley (if desired) and serve.
Enjoy!

Chapter 3: Appetizers

Tzatziki and Pita Chips

Ingredients:
1 cup plain Greek yogurt
1/2 English cucumber, grated and squeezed of excess liquid
2 cloves of garlic, minced
2 tbsp chopped fresh dill
2 tbsp lemon juice
Salt and pepper to taste
4 pita breads
Olive oil for brushing

Directions:
In a mixing bowl, combine the Greek yogurt, grated cucumber, minced garlic, dill, lemon juice, salt, and pepper. Mix well.
Cover and refrigerate for at least 30 minutes to allow the flavors to meld.
Preheat the oven to 350°F (175°C) and line a baking sheet with parchment paper.
Cut each pita bread into 8 wedges.
Brush the wedges with olive oil and sprinkle with a pinch of salt.
Arrange the pita wedges on the prepared baking sheet.
Bake for 8-10 minutes or until the wedges are golden brown and crispy.
Remove from the oven and let them cool for a few minutes.
Serve the tzatziki with the pita chips.
Enjoy!

Chapter 3: Appetizers

Marinated Olives

Ingredients:
1/2 cup of mixed olives (such as Kalamata and green olives)
2 cloves of garlic, minced
1/4 teaspoon of red pepper flakes
2 tablespoons of olive oil
1 tablespoon of lemon juice
1/2 teaspoon of dried oregano
Salt and pepper, to taste

Directions:
In a small bowl, combine the olives, garlic, red pepper flakes, olive oil, lemon juice, and oregano. Stir to combine.
Season the marinade with salt and pepper to taste.
Cover the bowl with plastic wrap and refrigerate for at least 2 hours, or overnight, to allow the flavors to meld.
Serve the olives cold as an appetizer or snack.
Note: Feel free to adjust the amount of garlic, red pepper flakes, lemon juice, and oregano to your taste.

Chapter 3: Appetizers

Pepperoni and Cheese Roll-Ups

Ingredients:
4 slices of pepperoni
4 slices of cheese (cheddar or mozzarella)
1 sheet of puff pastry, thawed
1 egg, beaten (for egg wash)

Directions:
Preheat the oven to 400°F (200°C). Line a baking sheet with parchment paper.
Roll out the puff pastry sheet on a lightly floured surface until it is slightly larger.
Cut the puff pastry sheet into 4 equal squares.
Place 2 slices of pepperoni and 1 slice of cheese in the center of each square.
Fold the corners of the pastry squares up and
over the filling, pinching the edges to seal.
Place the roll-ups on the prepared baking sheet.
Brush the roll-ups with the beaten egg.
Bake the roll-ups for 12-15 minutes, or until they are puffed and golden brown.
Remove from the oven and let them cool for a couple of minutes before serving.
Note: You can also use other toppings such as ham, bacon, or vegetables.
You can also add some seasonings such as herbs or spices
to the puff pastry before rolling it out.
You can also add some dipping sauces like marinara or ranch for extra flavor.

Chapter 3: Appetizers

Baked Parmesan Garlic Fries

Ingredients:
1 lb. russet potatoes, sliced into fries
3 cloves of garlic, minced
1/4 cup grated Parmesan cheese
1 tsp. dried oregano
Salt and pepper, to taste
1 tbsp. olive oil

Directions:
Preheat the oven to 425 degrees F.
In a large bowl, toss the potatoes with olive oil, minced garlic, grated Parmesan cheese, dried oregano, salt, and pepper.
Spread the fries out on a baking sheet and bake for 25-30 minutes, or until golden brown and crispy.
Serve hot and enjoy!
Note : You can adjust the serving size as per your requirement.

Chapter 4: Dinner

One-pan roasted chicken and vegetables

Ingredients:
1 lb. boneless, skinless chicken breast
1 lb. mixed vegetables (such as carrots, potatoes,
bell peppers, onions, and broccoli)
1 tbsp. olive oil
1 tsp. dried thyme
Salt and pepper, to taste

Directions:
Preheat the oven to 400 degrees F.
In a large bowl, toss the vegetables with olive oil, dried thyme, salt, and pepper.
Arrange the vegetables in a single layer in a large baking dish.
Place the chicken breast on top of the vegetables.
Roast in the oven for 25-30 minutes, or until the chicken is
cooked through and the vegetables are tender.
Serve hot and enjoy!
Note : You can adjust the serving size as per your requirement and use vegetables
of your choice.

Chapter 4: Dinner

Skillet beef and broccoli

Ingredients:

8 oz. beef (sirloin or flank steak) sliced into thin strips
2 cups broccoli florets
1 tbsp. vegetable oil
1 clove garlic, minced
1 tbsp. soy sauce
- tbsp. oyster sauce
1 tsp. cornstarch
Salt and pepper, to taste

Directions:

Heat the vegetable oil in a arge skillet over high heat.
Season the beef with salt and pepper, add it to the skillet and cook until browned, about 2-3 minutes.
Remove the beef from the skillet and set it aside.
In the same skillet, add the broccoli, garlic, soy sauce, and oyster sauce.
Cook until the broccoli is tender, about 3-4 minutes.
In a small bowl, mix together the cornstarch and
1 tablespoon of water to make a slurry.
Add the beef back to the skillet and pour the cornstarch slurry over the beef and broccoli. Cook for an additional 2-3 minutes, or until the sauce has thickened.
Serve hot and enjoy!
Note : You can adjust the serving size as per your requirement, you can also add other vegetables of your choice like bell pepper, onion.

Chapter 4: Dinner

Grilled cheese and tomato soup

Ingredients:
2 slices of bread
2 slices of cheddar cheese
2 tbsp. butter
1 can of tomato soup
Salt and pepper, to taste

Directions:
Preheat a skillet over medium heat.
Place one slice of bread on a clean surface, add a slice of cheese on top and place the other slice of bread on top.
Spread butter on one side of sandwich and place it butter side down in skillet.
Spread butter on the other side and cook until the bread is golden brown and the cheese is melted.
Flip the sandwich and cook the other side until golden brown.
While the sandwich is cooking, heat up the tomato soup in a saucepan over medium heat.
Season with salt and pepper to taste.
Serve the grilled cheese with the tomato soup and enjoy!
Note : You can adjust the serving size as per your requirement, you can also use different types of cheese of your choice.

Chapter 4: Dinner

Spaghetti with marinara sauce

Ingredients:
8 oz. spaghetti
1 cup marinara sauce
1 tbsp. olive oil
1 clove garlic, minced
Salt and pepper, to taste
Optional: grated Parmesan cheese and chopped fresh basil for serving

Directions:
Bring a large pot of salted water to a boil. Add the spaghetti and cook according to package instructions until al dente.
Drain the spaghetti and set it aside.
In a large skillet over medium heat, add the olive oil and minced garlic.
Cook until fragrant, about 1-2 minutes.
Add the marinara sauce to the skillet and bring it to a simmer
Cook for about 5 minutes.
Add the cooked spaghetti to the skillet with the sauce and toss to coat the spaghetti evenly.
Season with salt and pepper to taste.
Serve with grated Parmesan cheese and chopped fresh basil (if desired)
Note : You can also add some vegetables or meat for more flavor.

Chapter 4: Dinner

Meatball sub

Ingredients:
4 meatballs (store-bought or homemade)
1 sub roll
1/4 cup marinara sauce
1/4 cup shredded mozzarella cheese
Salt and pepper, to taste

Directions:
Preheat the oven to 350 degrees F.
Cut the sub roll in half and place it on a baking sheet, cut side up.
Spread the marinara sauce on the bottom half of the roll.
Place the meatballs on top of the sauce and sprinkle
shredded mozzarella cheese over the meatballs.
Season with salt and pepper to taste.
Place the top half of the roll on top of the meatballs and cheese.
Bake in the preheated oven for 8-10 minutes or until the
bread is toasted and the cheese is melted.
you can also add some vegetables, like lettuce, onion, pickles and use different type
of cheese of your choice.
Serve hot and enjoy!

Chapter 4: Dinner

BBQ pulled pork sandwich

Ingredients:
8 oz. pork shoulder or butt
1/4 cup BBQ sauce
1 bun
Salt and pepper, to taste

Directions:
Preheat your oven to 300 degrees F.
Season the pork shoulder or butt with salt and pepper, then place it in a roasting pan or Dutch oven.
Cover the pan or Dutch oven with foil and place it in the oven.
Cook for about 4-5 hours or until the pork is tender and falls apart easily.
Remove the pan from the oven and let it cool slightly.
Shred the pork with a fork or your hands.
Heat a skillet over medium heat and add the shredded pork, pour BBQ sauce over the pork and stir to coat. Cook for 5-6 minutes.
Toast the bun in the skillet or in a toaster.
Assemble the sandwich by placing the pork on the bottom half of the bun.
you can also add some vegetables, like lettuce, onion, pickles and use different type of cheese of your choice.
Serve hot and enjoy!

Chapter 4: Dinner

Baked salmon with lemon and herbs

Ingredients:
4 oz. salmon fillet
1 tbsp. olive oil
1/2 lemon, juiced
1 tsp. chopped fresh herbs (such as parsley, thyme, or dill)
Salt and pepper, to taste

Directions:
Preheat the oven to 425 degrees F.
Line a baking sheet with parchment paper.
Place the salmon fillet on the prepared baking sheet.
Brush the salmon with olive oil and squeeze the lemon juice over the top.
Sprinkle the chopped herbs, salt, and pepper over the salmon.
Bake in the preheated oven for 12-15 minutes, or until the salmon is cooked through and the flesh is opaque.
Serve hot and enjoy!
Note : You can also add some vegetables, like broccoli, asparagus, or green beans, to make it a complete meal.

Chapter 4: Dinner

Crispy chicken tenders with honey mustard dipping sauce

Ingredients:
8 oz. chicken tenders
1/2 cup flour, 1 tsp. paprika, 1 tsp. garlic powder, salt, pepper
1 egg
1 cup panko bread crumbs
1/4 cup vegetable oil

Directions:
Mix flour, paprika, garlic powder, salt, and pepper in a shallow dish.
Beat the egg in another shallow dish.
Place panko in a third shallow dish.
Coat chicken in flour mixture, egg, and panko.
Heat vegetable oil in skillet and cook chicken on medium-high
until golden brown and crispy (2-3 min per side)
Serve with Honey Mustard Dipping Sauce: -2 tbsp. Dijon mustard -2 tbsp. honey -1 tbsp. olive oil -1 tbsp. apple cider vinegar , mix well. Salt and pepper, to taste

Chapter 4: Dinner

Chicken and vegetable stir-fry

Ingredients:
4 oz boneless, skinless chicken breast, sliced
1 cup mixed vegetables (such as bell peppers, onions, carrots, broccoli)
1 tablespoon vegetable oil
1 clove garlic, minced
1 tablespoon soy sauce
1/2 tablespoon cornstarch
Salt and pepper, to taste

Directions:
Heat a large skillet or wok over high heat. Add the vegetable oil.
Add the chicken and stir-fry for 2-3 minutes or until cooked through.
Remove the chicken from the skillet and set it aside.
Add the vegetables, garlic, and soy sauce to the skillet and stir-fry for 3-4 minutes or until the vegetables are tender.
In a small bowl, mix together the cornstarch and 1/2 tablespoon of water to make a slurry.
Add the chicken back to the skillet and pour the cornstarch slurry over the chicken and vegetables. Cook for an additional 2-3 minutes, or until the sauce has thickened.
Serve hot and enjoy!
Note: You can also use vegetables of your choice and adjust the seasoning to your liking.

Chapter 4: Dinner

Ground Meat chili with Crackers

Ingredients:

8 oz. ground meat (beef, pork, turkey or chicken)
1 can diced tomatoes (14.5 oz)
1 can red kidney beans (14.5 oz) drained and rinsed
1 onion, diced
1 green bell pepper, diced
2 cloves of garlic, minced
1 tbsp. chili powder
1 tsp. cumin powder
Salt and pepper, to taste
Crackers for serving

Directions:

In a large pot or Dutch oven, cook the ground meat over medium-high heat until browned, about 5-7 minutes.
Drain off any excess fat.
Add the onion, green bell pepper, and garlic to the pot and cook until softened, about 3-5 minutes.
Stir in the diced tomatoes, kidney beans, chili powder, cumin powder, salt and pepper.
Bring the chili to a simmer and let cook for about 15-20 minutes, or until the vegetables are tender and the flavors have melded together.
you can also add some more vegetables or beans of your choice, also you can adjust the spiciness level according to your taste.
Serve hot with crackers and enjoy!

Chapter 4: Dinner

Baked salmon with a honey mustard glaze

Ingredients:
4 oz salmon fillet
1 tbsp olive oil
1 tbsp honey
1 tbsp dijon mustard
1 tsp lemon juice
Salt and pepper, to taste

Directions:
Preheat the oven to 375 degrees F.
Line a baking sheet with parchment paper.
Place the salmon fillet on the prepared baking sheet.
In a small bowl, mix together the olive oil, honey, Dijon mustard, lemon juice, and a pinch of salt and pepper.
Brush the honey mustard mixture over the salmon.
Bake in the preheated oven for 12-15 minutes, or until the salmon is cooked through and the flesh is opaque.
you can also add some vegetables, like broccoli, asparagus, or green beans, to make it a complete meal.
Serve hot and enjoy!

Chapter 4: Dinner

Cheddar and broccoli omelette

Ingredients:
2 large eggs
1/4 cup milk
Salt and pepper, to taste
1/2 cup finely chopped broccoli florets
1/4 cup shredded cheddar cheese
1 tsp butter

Directions:
Whisk together the eggs, milk, salt, and pepper in a small bowl.
Heat a small skillet over medium heat and add butter.
Once the butter is melted, add the chopped broccoli florets and stir-fry for a minute or two until they are tender.
Pour the egg mixture over the broccoli and cook for about 1-2 minutes or until the edges start to set.
Sprinkle shredded cheddar cheese over one half of the omelet.
Use a spatula to fold the other half of the omelet over the cheese and cook for an additional 1-2 minutes or until the cheese is melted and the eggs are cooked through. You can also add some vegetables or meat of your choice, also you can use different types of cheese of your choice.
Serve hot and enjoy!

Chapter 4: Dinner

Creamy chicken and mushroom pasta

Ingredients:
8 oz. of boneless, skinless chicken breast, cut into bite-sized pieces
1 cup of sliced mushrooms
1/4 cup of heavy cream
1/4 cup of grated Parmesan cheese
2 cloves of garlic, minced
2 tbsp of butter
Salt and pepper, to taste
8 oz. of linguine or fettuccine pasta
Fresh parsley, chopped (optional)

Directions:
Cook the pasta according to package instructions until al dente.
Drain and set aside.
In a large skillet, melt the butter over medium-high heat.
Add the garlic and sauté until fragrant.
Add the chicken and mushrooms, and cook until the chicken is no longer pink.
Reduce the heat to low, and add the heavy cream and Parmesan cheese.
Stir until the cheese is melted and the sauce is creamy.
Season with salt and pepper to taste.
Add the cooked pasta to the skillet and toss to coat with the sauce.
Serve hot and garnish with chopped parsley if desired.

Chapter 4: Dinner

Beef burritos with salsa

Ingredients:

1 lb beef (ground or thinly sliced)
1 onion, diced
1 bell pepper, diced
1 can black beans, drained and rinsed
1 cup salsa
1 tsp cumin
Salt and pepper to taste
8-10 flour or corn tortillas
Optional toppings: shredded cheese, sour cream, avocado, cilantro

Directions:

In a large skillet, brown the beef over medium-high heat.
Drain any excess fat.
Add the onion and bell pepper to the skillet and cook until softened.
Stir in the black beans, salsa, cumin, salt, and pepper.
Cook for an additional 5 minutes, or until heated through.
Warm the tortillas in the oven or on a stovetop griddle.
To assemble the burritos, place a few spoonful's of the beef mixture in the center of each tortilla, and top with any additional toppings of your choice.
Fold the sides of the tortilla in towards the center and roll it up tightly.
Serve warm and Enjoy your burrito with salsa
Note: You can also add some diced tomatoes ,lettuce, or any other toppings to make it more delicious.

Chapter 4: Dinner

Chicken fajitas

Ingredients:

1 lb boneless, skinless chicken breast, thinly sliced
1 onion, sliced
1 bell pepper, sliced
1 tbsp vegetable oil
2 tsp fajita seasoning
Salt and pepper to taste
8-10 flour or corn tortillas
Optional toppings: shredded cheese, sour cream, avocado, salsa, lime wedges

Directions:

In a large bowl, toss the chicken, onion, and bell pepper with the vegetable oil, fajita seasoning, salt, and pepper.
Heat a large skillet over medium-high heat. Add the chicken mixture and cook, stirring occasionally, until the chicken is cooked through and the vegetables are softened, about 8-10 minutes.
Warm the tortillas in the oven or on a stovetop griddle.
To assemble the fajitas, place a few spoonful of the chicken mixture in the center of each tortilla, and top with any additional toppings of your choice.
Fold the sides of the tortilla in towards the center and roll it up tightly.
Serve warm and Enjoy your delicious fajitas!
Note: You can also add some diced tomatoes, lettuce, or any other toppings to make it more delicious.

Chapter 4: Dinner

Spinach and Monterrey Jack Cheese Omelet

Ingredients:
2 large eggs
2 tbsp. milk
Salt and pepper to taste
2 tbsp. butter
1/2 cup fresh spinach, chopped
1/4 cup Monterey Jack cheese, shredded

Directions:
In a small bowl, whisk together the eggs, milk, salt, and pepper.
Heat a non-stick skillet over medium heat. Add the butter and let it melt.
Pour the egg mixture into the skillet and cook for
2-3 minutes, or until the edges start to set.
Add the spinach to one half of the omelet and sprinkle the cheese on top.
Carefully fold the other half of the omelet over the spinach and cheese.
Cook for an additional 1-2 minutes, or until the cheese is melted
and the eggs are cooked to your liking.
Serve and enjoy your Spinach and Monterey Jack Cheese Omelet!
Note: You can add some diced tomatoes, mushrooms or any other
vegetables to make it more delicious.

Chapter 4: Dinner
Chicken Fettuccini Noodles

Ingredients:
8 oz. fettuccine noodles
1 boneless, skinless chicken breast
2 cloves of garlic, minced
1 tbsp butter
1/4 cup heavy cream
1/4 cup grated parmesan cheese
Salt and pepper, to taste
Optional: chopped parsley for garnish

Directions:
Cook the fettuccine noodles according to package instructions until al dente. Drain and set aside.
While the noodles are cooking, season the chicken breast with salt and pepper. Heat a skillet over medium-high heat and add the chicken. Cook for about 6-7 minutes per side, or until cooked through. Remove from skillet and slice into bite-sized pieces.
In the same skillet, add the butter and garlic. Cook until fragrant, about 1-2 minutes.
Add the heavy cream and parmesan cheese to the skillet and stir until the cheese is melted and the sauce is smooth.
Add the cooked and sliced chicken to the skillet and toss to coat with the sauce.
Add the cooked fettuccine noodles to the skillet and toss to combine.
Serve and garnish with chopped parsley, if desired. Enjoy!

Chapter 4: Dinner

Lemon and herb baked chicken breast

Ingredients:
4 boneless, skinless chicken breasts
2 tbsp olive oil
2 cloves of garlic, minced
1/4 cup fresh parsley, chopped
1/4 cup fresh basil, chopped
2 tbsp fresh thyme, chopped
1/4 cup fresh lemon juice
Salt and pepper to taste

Directions:
Preheat the oven to 375°F (190°C).
In a small bowl, mix together the olive oil, garlic, parsley, basil, thyme, lemon juice, salt, and pepper.
Place the chicken breasts in a baking dish, and brush the mixture over the chicken.
Bake for 25-30 minutes, or until the chicken is cooked through.
Remove from the oven and let it cool for a few minutes.
Serve and enjoy your Lemon and Herb Baked Chicken Breast!
Note: You can also add some diced vegetables like zucchini, bell pepper, or any other vegetables to make it more delicious and healthy.

Chapter 4: Dinner

Chicken Parmesan

Ingredients:

1 boneless, skinless chicken breast
1/2 cup all-purpose flour
1 egg, beaten
1/2 cup breadcrumbs
1/4 cup grated parmesan cheese
1/4 tsp salt and 1/4 tsp pepper
1/4 cup marinara sauce
1/2 cup shredded mozzarella cheese

Directions:

Preheat oven to 375°F (190°C).
In a shallow dish, combine the flour, salt and pepper.
In another shallow dish, beat the egg.
In a third shallow dish, mix together breadcrumbs and grated parmesan cheese.
Cut the chicken breast in half, width-wise so you have 2 thin cutlets.
Dredge each chicken cutlet in the flour mixture, then the egg mixture, and then the breadcrumb mixture, making sure to press the
breadcrumbs onto the chicken to adhere.
Place the chicken cutlets on a baking sheet lined with parchment paper.
Bake for 20-25 minutes, or until the chicken is cooked through.
Remove the chicken from the oven and top each cutlet with marinara
sauce and shredded mozzarella cheese.
Return to the oven and bake for an additional 5-7 minutes, or
until the cheeseis melted and bubbly.
Serve with spaghetti noodles and enjoy your Chicken Parmesan!

Chapter 4: Dinner

Baked macaroni and cheese with bacon

Ingredients:
1 cup elbow macaroni
1/4 cup butter
1/4 cup all-purpose flour
2 cups milk
1 cup shredded cheddar cheese
1/4 cup grated parmesan cheese
Salt and pepper to taste
1/4 cup cooked bacon, crumbled

Directions:
Preheat the oven to 375°F (190°C).
Cook the macaroni according to package instructions. Drain and set aside.
In a medium saucepan, melt the butter over medium heat.
Stir in the flour and cook for 1-2 minutes, or until the mixture turns golden brown.
Gradually whisk in the milk and bring the mixture to a boil.
Reduce the heat to low and stir in the cheddar cheese, parmesan cheese, salt, and pepper until the cheese is melted and the sauce is smooth.
Stir in the cooked macaroni and crumbled bacon.
Pour the macaroni and cheese mixture into an oven-safe baking dish.
Bake for 15-20 minutes, or until the cheese is bubbly and the top is golden brown.
Serve and enjoy your Baked Macaroni and Cheese with Bacon!
Note: You can also add some diced vegetables like broccoli, peas, or any other vegetables to make it more delicious and healthy.

Chapter 5: Desserts

Chocolate chip cookies

Ingredients:
1 cup all-purpose flour
1/2 cup granulated sugar
1/2 cup brown sugar
1/2 cup unsalted butter, at room temperature
1 egg
1 tsp vanilla extract
1 cup semisweet chocolate chips

Directions:
Preheat your oven to 350°F (175°C) and line a baking sheet with parchment paper.
In a large mixing bowl, cream together the butter, granulated sugar, and brown sugar until smooth.
Beat in the egg and vanilla extract.
Gradually mix in the flour until just combined.
Stir in the chocolate chips.
Using a cookie scoop or spoon, drop the dough onto the prepared baking sheet, spacing them about 2 inches apart.
Bake for 10-12 minutes, or until the edges are golden brown.
Remove from the oven and let the cookies cool on the baking sheet for 5 minutes before transferring them to a wire rack to cool completely.
Enjoy your homemade chocolate chip cookies!

Chapter 5: Desserts

Apple crisp

Ingredients:
1 apple, peeled, cored and chopped into small pieces
1 tbsp granulated sugar
1/4 tsp ground cinnamon
1 tbsp rolled oats
1 tbsp brown sugar
1 tsp unsalted butter

Directions:
Preheat your oven to 350°F (175°C) and grease a small baking dish or ramekin.
In a mixing bowl, combine the chopped apple,
granulated sugar, and cinnamon. Mix well.
Transfer the apple mixture to the prepared baking dish.
In the same mixing bowl, combine the rolled oats, brown sugar, and butter.
Mix well and sprinkle the mixture over the apples.
Place the baking dish on a baking sheet and bake in the preheated oven for 25-30 minutes or until the top is golden brown and the apples are tender.
Remove from the oven and let it cool for a few minutes before serving.
Can be served warm or cold.
Enjoy your homemade apple crisp!

Chapter 5: Desserts

Banana bread

Ingredients:
1 cup all-purpose flour
1 tsp baking powder
1/4 tsp baking soda
1/4 tsp salt
2 ripe bananas, mashed
1/2 cup granulated sugar
1 egg
1/4 cup unsalted butter, melted

Directions:
Preheat your oven to 350°F (175°C) and grease a loaf pan.
In a medium mixing bowl, whisk together the flour,
baking powder, baking soda, and salt.
In a separate large mixing bowl, mash the bananas with a fork or potato masher.
Add the sugar, egg, and melted butter to the mashed bananas and mix well.
Gradually stir in the dry ingredients until just combined.
Pour the batter into the prepared loaf pan.
Bake in the preheated oven for 50-60 minutes or until a toothpick or cake tester
inserted into the center comes out clean.
Remove from the oven and let the banana bread cool
in the pan for 10 minutes before
transferring it to a wire rack to cool completely.
Enjoy your homemade banana bread!

Chapter 5: Desserts

Chocolate mousse

Ingredients:
1/4 cup semisweet chocolate chips
1 egg, separated
2 tbsp granulated sugar

Directions:
Melt the chocolate chips in the microwave or over a double boiler. Set aside and let it cool for a few minutes.
In a separate mixing bowl, beat the egg white until stiff peaks form.
In another mixing bowl, beat the egg yolk and sugar together until light and fluffy.
Gradually mix in the melted chocolate.
Gently fold in the beaten egg whites.
Spoon the mixture into a small ramekin or glass.
Chill in the refrigerator for at least 1 hour, or until set.
Enjoy your homemade chocolate mousse!

Chapter 5: Desserts

Berry sorbet

Ingredients:
1/2 cup mixed berries (such as strawberries, raspberries, or blueberries)
2 tbsp granulated sugar
2 tbsp water

Directions:
In a blender, puree the berries, sugar, and water until smooth.
Taste and add more sugar if needed.
Pour the mixture into a container and freeze for at least 1 hour, or until firm.
Remove the sorbet from the freezer and let it sit at room temperature
for a few minutes before scooping and serving.
Enjoy your homemade berry sorbet!

Note: you can use any type of berries you have available, if you don't have fresh berries you can use frozen.

Chapter 5: Desserts

Lemon bars

Ingredients:
1/2 cup all-purpose flour
1/4 cup powdered sugar, plus extra for dusting
1/4 cup unsalted butter, at room temperature
2 tbsp lemon juice
2 tbsp granulated sugar

Directions:
Preheat your oven to 350°F (175°C) and grease a 8x8 inch square baking dish.
In a mixing bowl, combine the flour, powdered sugar, and butter.
Mix until the mixture resembles coarse crumbs.
Press the mixture into the prepared baking dish and bake for
15-20 minutes or until the edges are golden brown.
Remove from the oven and let it cool for a few minutes.
In the same mixing bowl, combine the lemon juice and granulated sugar.
Pour the mixture over the cooled crust.
Bake for an additional 20-25 minutes or until the filling is set.
Remove from the oven and let it cool completely.
Dust the top with powdered sugar before cutting into squares and serving.
Enjoy your homemade lemon bars!

Chapter 5: Desserts

Brownies

Ingredients:
1/4 cup all-purpose flour
1/4 cup unsweetened cocoa powder
1/4 cup granulated sugar
1/4 cup unsalted butter, melted
1 egg

Directions:
Preheat your oven to 350°F (175°C) and grease an 8x8 inch square baking dish.
In a mixing bowl, combine the flour, cocoa powder, sugar, melted butter, and egg. Mix until well combined.
Pour the mixture into the prepared baking dish.
Bake in the preheated oven for 20-25 minutes or until a toothpick inserted into the center comes out clean.
Remove from the oven and let it cool completely before cutting into squares and serving.
Enjoy your homemade brownies!

Chapter 5: Desserts

Peach cobbler

Ingredients:
1 cup sliced peeled peaches
2 tbsp granulated sugar
1 tbsp all-purpose flour
1/4 tsp ground cinnamon
1/4 cup all-purpose flour
2 tbsp granulated sugar
1 tbsp unsalted butter, at room temperature
1/4 tsp baking powder

Directions:
Preheat your oven to 350°F (175°C) and grease a small baking dish or ramekin.
In a mixing bowl, combine the peaches, 2 tablespoons
of sugar, 1 tablespoon of flour, and cinnamon. Mix well.
Transfer the peach mixture to the prepared baking dish.
In the same mixing bowl, combine 1/4 cup of flour, 2 tablespoons of sugar, butter, and baking powder. Mix well and sprinkle the mixture over the peaches.
Place the baking dish on a baking sheet and bake in the preheated oven for 25-30 minutes or until the top is golden brown and the peaches are tender.
Remove from the oven and let it cool for a few minutes before serving.
Can be served warm or cold.
Enjoy your homemade peach cobbler!

Chapter 5: Desserts

Chocolate covered strawberries

Ingredients:
1/4 cup semisweet chocolate chips
8-10 fresh strawberries with stem

Directions:
Rinse and dry the strawberries.
Melt the chocolate chips in the microwave or over a double boiler.
Dip the strawberries into the melted chocolate, using a
toothpick or fork to hold onto the stem.
Place the chocolate covered strawberries on a parchment-lined baking sheet.
Chill in the refrigerator for at least 30 minutes to set the chocolate.
Once the chocolate is set, the strawberries can be served and enjoyed.
Enjoy your chocolate covered strawberries!

Chapter 5: Desserts

Cheesecake

Ingredients:
1/4 cup graham cracker crumbs
2 tbsp granulated sugar
2 tbsp unsalted butter, melted
8 oz cream cheese, at room temperature
1/4 cup granulated sugar
1 egg

Directions:
Preheat your oven to 325°F (165°C) and grease a 9-inch springform pan.
In a mixing bowl, combine the graham cracker crumbs,
2 tablespoons of sugar, and melted butter. Mix well.
Press the mixture into the bottom of the prepared springform pan.
In another mixing bowl, beat the cream cheese and 1/4 cup of sugar
until smooth. Beat in the egg.
Pour the cream cheese mixture over the crust in the pan.
Place the pan on a baking sheet and bake in the preheated
oven for 25-30 minutes or until the filling is set.
Remove from the oven and let it cool completely.
Chill in the refrigerator for at least 2 hours before serving.
Enjoy your homemade cheesecake!
Note: you can add any flavor you like to the cheesecake, like vanilla extract, lemon juice, etc

Chapter 5: Desserts

Microwave mug cake

Ingredients:

4 tablespoons all-purpose flour
4 tablespoons granulated sugar
2 tablespoons unsweetened cocoa powder
1/8 teaspoon baking powder
a pinch of salt
3 tablespoons milk
3 tablespoons vegetable oil
1/4 teaspoon vanilla extract

Directions:

In a microwave-safe mug, mix together the flour, sugar, cocoa powder, baking powder, and salt.
Stir in the milk, vegetable oil, and vanilla extract until the batter is smooth.
Microwave on high for 1 minute and 30 seconds, or until the cake has risen and is set in the middle.
Let the mug cake cool for a minute before eating. Enjoy!
Note: You can adjust the cooking time based on the wattage of your microwave. It may take longer or shorter time.

Chapter 5: Desserts

No-bake chocolate peanut butter bars

Ingredients:
1 cup graham cracker crumbs
1/2 cup powdered sugar
1/2 cup smooth peanut butter
1/2 cup unsalted butter, melted
1/2 cup semisweet chocolate chips
1/4 cup heavy cream

Directions:
In a mixing bowl, combine the graham cracker crumbs, powdered sugar, peanut butter, and melted butter. Mix well.
Press the mixture into the bottom of a square pan lined with parchment paper.
In a microwave-safe bowl, combine the chocolate chips and heavy cream. Microwave in 30-second increments, stirring after each increment, until the chocolate is fully melted and smooth.
Pour the melted chocolate over the peanut butter crust and spread it evenly.
Refrigerate the bars for at least 2 hours, or until the chocolate is fully set.
Once set, cut the bars into squares and enjoy!
These bars can be stored in an airtight container in the refrigerator for up to a week.
You can enjoy them as a snack or a dessert.

Chapter 5: Desserts

Berries with yogurt

Ingredients:

1 cup mixed berries (such as strawberries, blueberries, raspberries, and blackberries)
1 cup plain yogurt
1 tablespoon honey (optional)

Directions:

Wash and dry the berries, then place them in a bowl.
In a separate bowl, mix together the yogurt and honey, if using.
Pour the yogurt mixture over the berries and stir gently to combine.
Transfer the berry and yogurt mixture to a serving bowl or individual bowls.
Enjoy immediately or refrigerate for later.
This is a simple, healthy and delicious recipe that can be easily prepared by a single man. Berries are packed with antioxidants and vitamins, while yogurt provides protein and probiotics. You can also add some granola or chopped nuts for extra crunch.

Chapter 5: Desserts

Strawberry ice cream

Ingredients:
1 cup fresh strawberries, hulled and roughly chopped
1/2 cup granulated sugar
1 cup heavy cream
1 cup whole milk
1 teaspoon vanilla extract

Directions:
In a blender or food processor, puree the strawberries until smooth.
In a medium saucepan over medium heat, combine the strawberry puree, sugar, cream, milk, and vanilla extract.
Cook, stirring occasionally, until the mixture is hot and the sugar has dissolved.
Remove from heat and allow to cool completely.
Once cooled, pour the mixture into an ice cream maker and churn according to the manufacturer's instructions.
Once churned, transfer the ice cream to a container, and freeze for at least 4 hours or overnight.
Scoop out the ice cream and enjoy it!
This recipe is a simple and delicious way for a single man to make homemade strawberry ice cream. You can also add other ingredients like lemon zest or chocolate chips to change the flavor.
Note: If you don't have an ice cream maker, you can also use a Ziploc bag and a mixture of ice and salt to churn the mixture

Chapter 5: Desserts

Chocolate covered banana

Ingredients:
1 banana
1/2 cup semisweet chocolate chips
1 teaspoon vegetable oil (optional)
Toppings of your choice (such as chopped nuts, shredded coconut, or sprinkles)

Directions:
Peel the banana and cut it in half, then insert a popsicle stick into each half.
Place the bananas on a baking sheet lined with
parchment paper, and freeze for at least 1 hour.
In a microwave-safe bowl, combine the chocolate chips and vegetable oil, if using.
Microwave in 30-second increments, stirring after each
increment, until the chocolate is fully melted and smooth.
Remove the bananas from the freezer.
Hold the banana by the stick and dip it into the
melted chocolate, making sure to coat it evenly.
Place the chocolate-covered banana back on the baking sheet, and
immediately add your desired toppings.
Return the bananas to the freezer for at least 30 minutes,
or until the chocolate is fully set.
Once set, remove the bananas from the freezer and enjoy!
This is a fun and easy recipe for a single man to make at home. Chocolate covered bananas are a delicious and healthy treat. You can also try different type of chocolate to get different flavor.

Chapter 5: Desserts

Lemon poppy seed muffins

Ingredients:
1 cup all-purpose flour
1/4 cup granulated sugar
1 tsp baking powder
1 tbsp poppy seeds
1/4 cup unsalted butter, melted
1 egg
2 tbsp lemon juice

Directions:
Preheat your oven to 350°F (175°C) and line a muffin tin with paper liners.
In a mixing bowl, combine the flour, sugar, baking powder, and poppy seeds.
In another mixing bowl, whisk together the melted butter, egg, and lemon juice.
Gradually stir the wet ingredients into the dry ingredients until just combined.
Scoop the batter into the prepared muffin tin, filling each cup about 2/3 full.
Bake in the preheated oven for 20-25 minutes or until a toothpick inserted into the center of a muffin comes out clean.
Remove the muffins from the oven and let them cool in the pan for 5 minutes before transferring them to a wire rack to cool completely.
Enjoy your homemade lemon poppy seed muffins!

Recipe Index:

Apple crisp-89
Avocado toast with scrambled eggs-9
Bagel with tomato, avocado and bacon-23
Banana bread-90
Berry sorbet-92
Berries with yogurt-100
Black bean and sweet potato burrito-31
Blueberry pancakes-15
Baked Brie-52
Baked macaroni and cheese with bacon-87
Baked Parmesan Garlic Fries-67
Baked salmon with lemon and herbs-74
Baked salmon with a honey mustard glaze-78
BBQ Chicken Sandwich-41
BBQ pulled pork sandwich-73
Beef burritos with salsa-81
Breakfast burrito with scrambled eggs and veggies-12
Breakfast hash with sweet potatoes, bacon, and eggs-22
Breakfast potatoes with eggs and bacon-20
Breakfast pizza with sausage, egg, and cheese-24
Breakfast sandwich with bacon, egg, and cheese-17
Breakfast wrap with sausage, egg, and cheese-27
Broccoli and cheddar soup-36
Brownies-94
Buffalo Chicken Dip-60
Caprese Salad Skewers-50
Cheddar and broccoli omelette-79
Cheesecake-97
Cheesy Garlic Bread-51
Chicken and vegetable curry-37
Chicken and Vegetable stir-fry-76
Chicken fajitas -82
Chicken Parmesan-86
Chia seed pudding with almond milk and fruit-25
Chocolate chip cookies-88

Recipe Index:

Chocolate covered banana-102
Chocolate covered strawberries-96
Chocolate mousse-91
Cream Cheese Stuffed Jalapenos-53
Creamy chicken and mushroom pasta-80
Crispy chicken tenders with honey mustard dipping sauce-75
Cucumber and Dill Tea Sandwiches-58
Deviled Eggs-48
English muffin with ham and cheese-14
Fried Green Beans-59
French toast with fresh fruit-19
Greek salad with grilled chicken-32
Greek yogurt with berries and honey-10
Grilled cheese and tomato soup-70
Chicken Fettuccini Noodles-84
Grilled Chicken Caesar Salad-28
Grilled chicken and vegetable pasta-43
Grilled chicken and veggie kabobs-39
Guacamole and Chips-49
Ground Meat chili with Crackers-77
Lemon and herb baked chicken breast-85
Lemon bars-93
Lemon poppy seed muffins-103
Marinated Olives-65
Meatball sub-72
Mini Meatballs-55
Microwave mug cake-98
No-bake chocolate peanut butter bars-99
Oatmeal with nuts, seeds, and dried fruit-26
One-pan roasted chicken and vegetables-68
Omelet with mushrooms, peppers, and onions-13
Pesto and Ricotta Crostini-63

Recipe Index:

Peach cobbler-95
Peanut butter and banana smoothie-11
Pepperoni and Cheese Roll-Ups-66
Prosciutto Wrapped Melon-57
Quinoa and veggie stir-fry-33
Quinoa bowls with eggs, veggies, and avocado-16
Scrambled eggs with spinach and feta-8
Shrimp Cocktail-61
Skillet beef and broccoli-69
Smoked Salmon and Cream Cheese-62
Smoothie bowl with yogurt, berries, and granola-18
Spaghetti with marinara sauce-71
Spinach and feta omelet-35
Spinach and Feta Spanakopita-56
Spinach and Monterrey Jack Cheese Omelet-83
Strawberry ice cream-101
Stuffed Mushrooms-54
Tuna salad sandwich-30
Turkey and avocado lettuce cups-44
Turkey and cheese panini with pesto-47
Turkey and cheese quesadilla-42
Turkey and cheese wrap with avocado and tomato-29
Turkey and veggie stir fry with brown rice-46
Turkey and cheese melt with tomato soup-45
Turkey burger with sweet potato fries-34
Turkey chili with avocado-38
Turkey meatloaf with roasted vegetables-40
Tzatziki and Pita Chips-64
Yogurt parfait with granola and fruit

Printed in Great Britain
by Amazon

5836bd37-4e24-4e83-85d1-4c19e6ec5ffcR01